Contents

Any words appearing **like this**, are explained in the Glossary.

What are beetles?

Beetles are **insects**. They have six legs and two pairs of wings. There are thousands of different types of beetle.

Beetles can be found in many different sizes, shapes and colours. The weevil in the picture is a kind of beetle. **Ladybirds** are types of beetle.

What do beetles look like?

Beetles have very hard skins. Most beetles have four wings. Two are very tough. They fold over the **transparent** flying wings to protect them.

They have two **feelers** on their heads.
Their large eyes are actually many
small eyes side by side. Beetles are
mainly black, brown or green.

How big are beetles?

The largest beetle is called the Goliath
beetle. It can be as large as a man's
fist. It weighs about 100 grams, which
is the same as a small apple.

Most beetles are about as big as your
thumbnail but the smallest are tiny.
They are smaller than a dot made
with a pencil.

How are beetles born?

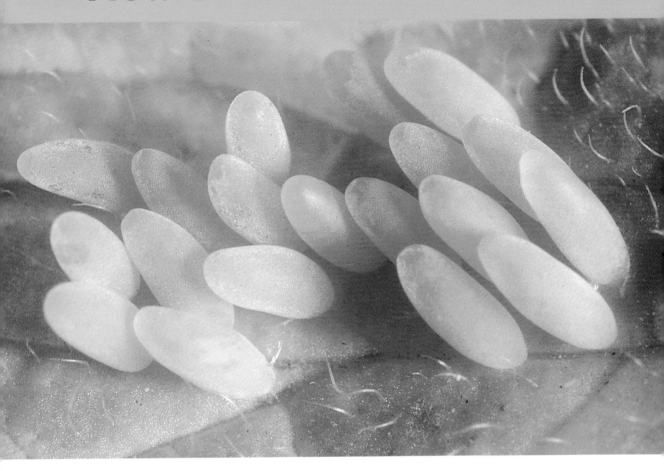

Some beetles are born in spring. Other types are born in autumn. Most **female** beetles lay many eggs. The eggs can be laid on the ground, on leaves, or in hollows in the ground.

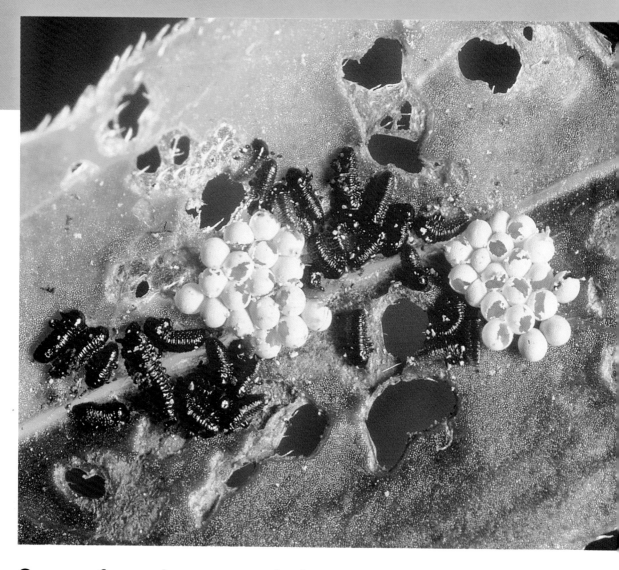

Some females guard the eggs until they **hatch**. When the eggs hatch, **larvae** crawl out. Most larvae have six legs but weevil larvae do not have any legs.

How do beetles grow?

Beetle **larvae** are like fleshy grubs.
They eat as fast as they can. When
they have grown larger they **moult**.
The old skin breaks, the larva wriggles
out and a new larger skin grows.

The larva moults about three times.
Then it becomes a **pupa**. Inside the
pupa it grows wings and changes
slowly into an **adult**.

What do beetles eat?

Many beetles eat other **insects**, worms or snails. Some kill animals and others eat animals that are already dead. Some types of beetle eat plants or seeds.

Many beetles have large jaws with **mandibles** for gripping their food. Beetle **larvae** can be very fierce. Water beetle larvae can eat **tadpoles**.

Which animals eat beetles?

Birds, lizards and frogs eat beetles. They are safe from spiders because of their hard skins. Some beetles make noises to frighten their enemies away.

If the Bloody-nosed beetle is attacked it spurts red liquid out of its mouth to help it to escape. In some countries, people hunt some large beetles to make them into soup.

Where do beetles live?

There are beetles living in nearly every country on Earth. Some types live in grassland, in woodland, or on the edges of rivers and streams.

Some types of beetle can be found
down on the seashore and others near
the tops of the highest mountains.
Some share the nests of other **insects**.

How do beetles move?

Some beetles can run fast. They have long, thin legs. Other beetles have shorter, stronger legs for digging. Climbing beetles have claws or sticky pads on their feet for gripping.

Many beetles can fly, but they do not fly
for long. It has to be warm for many of
them to fly at all. Some have wings that
are not strong enough for flying.

How long do beetles live?

Beetles usually live for less than a year. Some are born in autumn and **hibernate** during the winter as a **larva** or **pupa**. After they have laid their eggs in spring they die.

Other beetles born in the autumn bury themselves in the ground or under the bark of trees. They sleep through the winter as **adults**.

What do beetles do?

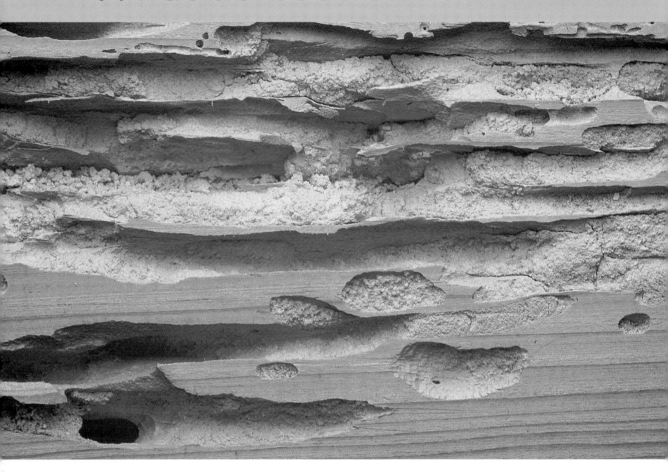

Many beetles spend their time under stones and logs. It is usually damp there and does not get too hot. Some live in people's houses and the **larvae** cause damage by eating the wood.

Some beetles bury themselves in sand or clay. **Dung** beetles collect the dung from bigger animals. They roll it away in balls and lay an egg in each ball.

How are beetles special?

There are more different kinds of beetle than any other type of animal. There are even beetles, with legs like paddles, which live in ponds.

Some special beetles even have other names. Glow-worms are not worms but beetles. Fireflies are not flies but beetles. They both make chemicals which can be seen in the dark.

Thinking about beetles

Where could you find beetles? Turn over some stones and small logs to see if any are underneath. Turn them back again carefully afterwards.

Why do you think they live there? Why is that the best place for them to be? What could happen to them if they were moved to some different places?

Bug map

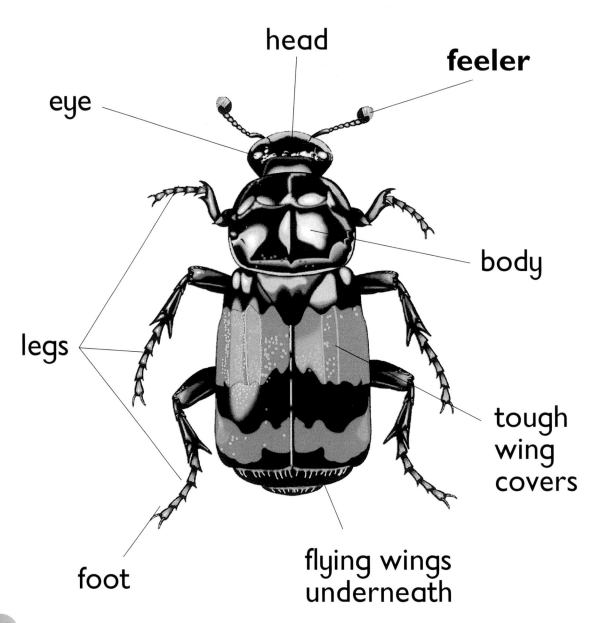

head

feeler

eye

body

legs

tough
wing
covers

foot

flying wings
underneath

Glossary

adult   a grown up

dung   the waste droppings which some animals leave behind

feelers   thin tubes that stick out from the head of an insect. They may be used to smell, feel or hear.

female   girl

hatch   come out of the egg

hibernate   sleep right through the winter

insects   small creatures with six legs

Ladybird   beetles which are usually red with black spots

larva   (more than one = larvae) the baby insect that hatches from the egg

mandibles   parts of the mouth of a beetle

moult   when an insect gets too big for its skin the old skin drops off and a new skin is underneath

pupa   (more than one = pupae) the larva makes a hard case around itself before it turns into an adult

tadpoles   frogs before they are grown up

transparent   you can see through it

Index